BREAKING THE HEX

life with God after the cross killed religion

Roger Fields and Jeff Fields

BROKEN EGG PRESS

Breaking the Hex is published by Broken Egg Press. For details on bulk sales contact Broken Egg Press at 2308 Lakeside Dr., Lexington, KY 40502.

ISBN: 1975909771
ISBN 13: 978-1975909772

Cover design: Dave Aldrich, www.aldrichdesign.com
Photos: Christopher Michael Images

This book is dedicated
to the memory of our dad.

Tom Fields

He consistently demonstrated God's
love and grace throughout our lives.

He made an eternal mark on us
and all of his grandchildren.

We think he would like this book.

what people are saying about this book

In this book, the Holy Spirit has led in articulating an old truth in unorthodox ways that will appeal to both the older and younger generations. However, the experienced cross (Gal.2:20) is little taught in today's church which, too, tends to obscure it to both!

CHARLES R. SOLOMON, Ed.D. author of Handbook to Happiness (Tyndale)

The Fields Brothers have crafted a unique tool to remind you not to fall for the lies of religious performance but to continue to rest in God's provision of grace and relationship. You'll enjoy the simplicity, the humor, and the wisdom in these pages.

WAYNE JACOBSEN, author of *He Loves Me*, *Finding Church*. Co-author of *The Shack*

Gee whiz, I really liked this book. It covers a lot of ground in a friendly, accessible way and unpacked a lot of baggage for me as a Christian with a serious "dead works" problem. Funny in places, like being given the straight dope by your smarter, cooler brother in others, it's a genuinely solid read. Typography and layout keep it light and fun while still delivering the intended message.

TROY DEVOLLD, TV Producer

My growth as a Christian began when I received an intimate, personal relationship with Jesus Christ. This book affirms that. Acting and being religious left me empty, obligated and unfulfilled. Thanks, Jeff and Roger, for helping me get back on track.

DOUG FLYNN, 2-time World Series Champion (1975,76 Cincinnati Reds) 1980 Gold Glove Award winner

---

Fabulous book! Almost every Christian believes that we are saved by grace but everything else is hard work...and this book exposes the danger of that theology. The book will be offensive to some who have spent their life and energy in the religious world. But the beauty is that every word is backed up by the Bible.

HON. TIM PHILPOT, Family Court Judge

This book will free your mind, heart and spirit.

MINDI THORE

Fantastic book! I see so many, many applications for its usage. First, for young people in the age levels from about 5th grade through community college age! Second, for new believers in their Small Group Study as it will lead to deeper sharing from scripture. But, what it does so very well is start from the "simple" and then allow for deeper investigation. Third, for people, regardless of age, who are struggling with grasping the "real truth" of who Christ is in them, and who they are in Christ, it will lead them to that understanding of their true identity.

LARRY COLEMAN, Bible Teacher, Teacher-Trainer, Speaker, Writer

———————————

My husband, Mark, is reading it, and he never reads books! He likes the short chapters and large print!

CARLA LAYTON

———————————

Just received it today and can not put it down!! Well I did have to go mow but came right back and picked it up again and again! See that is the thing, you don't have to read it straight through, but there is no rule to saying you can't, that is what I'm talking about! Religion, rules, list, rituals etc. etc. etc. This book I believe can help you find true freedom! Take a chance and take a look, I promise you will not be disappointed!! And then Pass it on!

KAYRENE LEWIS, Officer Manager

———————————

WOW! I am loving this book.

DIANNE BROOKS

———————————

Love this book! It is easy to read (great for people who do not like to read). It is fun to read. (You will find yourself laughing many times as you turn the pages!) But moreover, you will come to understand the deep and profound truth of what was accomplished when Jesus died on the Cross. Many believers actually are under a hex as I was for many years of my life, not understanding the "before" and "after" the Cross. I thought it was up to me to improve my life, to strive to be like Jesus! And I was so wrong! Guilt feelings of not "measuring up" and not "doing enough" disappear as you come to understand the true reality of God's love for you. "Breaking the Hex" is based on Gal. 3:1 and is truly a life-changing read.

CLARA FIELDS, Fields Brothers mom
(Thanks, mom!)

acknowledgments

Roger says, "THANKS!"

Thank you to my amazing wife, Lori, for having the vision for this book. Your passion for this project motivated me to do it. Your input gave me clarity. It would not have happened without your encouragement and prayers. I love you.

Thank you to my mom, Clara Fields, for always believing in me.

Thank you to my fabulous daughters: Terra Harrison, Mica Sims, Shannon Fields and Morgan Fields for making life so wonderful.

Thank you to Crystal Lince and Cody Danet for being part of my life. Your passion for living inspires me.

Thank you to Ken Dovey for your insight and passion. Thank you Bruce Chrouser for your spiritual wisdom that always challenges me.

Jeff says, "THANKS!"

Thanks to Mom for your love and support through the years. Thanks for encouraging us to know Christ as our life.

Thanks to our dear friends at Stanton Christian Church in Stanton, KY for your kindness and patience to a 21 year-old "pastor" and his wife many years ago.

Thanks to Landry, Jonathan, Angela, Troy, Josiah and Dawson. I love being your Dad.

Thanks to Nelson Akafuah, Jeff Bailey, and Casey Billings for your friendship and authentic conversations.

Thanks to Wayne Jacobsen and Brad Cummings for letting many of us listen in on your conversations through The God Journey podcasts.

Most of all, thanks to my incredible wife, Teresa, for your love and friendship for almost 35 years. I love you.

Special appreciation for editing to Dianne Brooks, Mark Cruse, Clara Fields, Joanna Fields, Lori Fields, Janet Huehls, Kay Lewis, Ande Long, Doug Money, and Bob Peterson.

TABLE OF CONTENTS

III. How God Made You New   113

IV. How Grace Sets You Free   143

obituary

Jerusalem – RELIGIOUS OBLIGATION, age 4,000+ years, died A.D. 30 on Golgotha Hill. "Religion" died of wounds while being publicly nailed to a cross with Jesus of Nazareth. Sadly and unnecessarily, survivors include performance, guilt, shame, pressure, fear and condemnation. Religion was a well-known and demanding taskmaster that led to pride and/or frustration. He was preceded in death by generations of well-intended, but self-righteous, people.

Memorial services will be held whenever those in Christ gather to remember the death of Jesus Christ. Supper will be served. Burial will be in the past, once and for all. Arrangements by Grace and Freedom.

Donations may be made (but are not recommended) to the First Church of Try-A-Little-Harder-Do-A-Little-More on Dead-End Street in Never-Enoughville.

so what's this hex?

You CRAZY Galatians!
Did someone put a HEX on you?

Galatians 3:1 (MSG)

Everything I thought I knew about
how to live the Christian life
turned out to be wrong.

(Everything. Wrong.)

I was clear about my eternal destiny.
Heaven is my home.
I understood I was forgiven
through faith in Jesus.
And I knew the Bible is inspired by God.
I got that down.

But I misunderstood "the Christian life,"
what it is and how to live it.

I thought I was saved by GRACE
but had to grow by EFFORT.

I thought I was supposed to MAKE it happen.

You know,
to be a follower of Jesus.
Disciple.
Mature Christian.

After receiving God's free gift of salvation
through Jesus, I thought
I was now obligated to do all the stuff
it seemed God expected of me.
And the list of stuff I thought I was
required to do kept growing.
Soon, my obligations as a Christian became a problem.

They crowded out everything
the Bible said I should be experiencing.

God's grace
Freedom
Love of God
Joy
Peace
Relationship with Jesus

Something was missing.
Something was wrong.
Really wrong.

The pressure of trying hard to live the Christian life began to suck
the life out of me. What was once joyful and energizing turned
into an obligation.
A big obligation.
An unsustainable obligation.

I focused on my own spiritual development.
I looked at diagrams that others said would help.
I followed principles I read in books.

After all, isn't that what I was
supposed to do?
Aren't we supposed to try hard to be like Jesus?
Aren't we supposed to follow Him?
Aren't we supposed to be a disciple?

Aren't we supposed to…?
Pray a lot
Read our Bible every day
Share our faith
Tithe regularly
Show up at some/most/all church services
Join a life group
Serve my local church
Listen to Christian music
Support world missions

Is this it? Is this why Jesus came?

Did Jesus leave Heaven, come to this earth, live a perfect life, endure a horrible crucifixion and rise from the dead so that we could live a life of never-ending Christian obligations? (Really?)

Did I misunderstand how this works? (YES.)
THAT is what this book is about.

It turns out I was under a **HEX**
and didn't know it.

And there is no freedom under the hex.
(HEAVENS TO BETSY!)

what Paul tells the Galatians...

How foolish can you be?
After starting your new lives in the
Spirit, why are you now
trying to become perfect by
YOUR OWN HUMAN EFFORT?

Galatians 3:3 (NLT)

THE GALATIAN COUNTY LINE

Welcome to Galatia County.

Galatia County is a nice place to visit but
you would NOT want to live there.

Galatia is a big county with numerous cities and towns.
It's doing well financially. Lots of hustle bustle.

There are lots of Christians here.
Several notable congregations.

(But there is a **BIG PROBLEM** here.)

You will find that the people here are religious.

They believe in Jesus. They know He is the Son of God. They understand that Jesus was crucified for their sins. They know He rose from the dead and ascended into Heaven.

The Christians in this county are under...well...a spell.
Some would call it a "curse." Others would call it a "hex."
No matter what you call it, it's not good.

It is odd, because the people here are not practicing the occult.
There are no psychics. No witchcraft. No fortune-telling. No crystal balls.
And yet...the Bible says they are under a hex.

How is that possible?

It turns out that the Christians in Galatia County are not doing anything weird. In fact, they are doing something almost every Christian does on a regular basis.

They are trying to add to the finished work of Jesus on the cross.

They don't know Jesus killed the way of religion on the cross.
They never saw the obituary.

They think if they
try a little harder,
do a little more,
then God will notice and bless
their extra commitment/dedication.

We call it the TRY-A-LITTLE-HARDER-DO-A-LITLLE-MORE SYNDROME.
Or as the book of Galatians calls it: "the hex."

They just think they can use their religious efforts to complete what Jesus started. They want to do stuff to get closer to God. No big deal.

(Scratch that!)

It's a **VERY BIG DEAL**!!!

Actually, they lived in the first century Roman empire so we don't know exactly how they were trying to do this. But we can easily speculate about how they would do it if they lived in our day.

They would have discipleship programs.
Christian life principles.
Bible reading plans.
Charts and diagrams to learn.
Services and schools to attend.
Ministry strategies to master.

And anything else to...
make them more like Jesus,
help them be better Christians,
grow them into spiritual maturity.

You see how this works?
Add-ons.
Do more stuff.
Press in.
Try harder.

Do NOT make your home in Galatia County.
This place will beat the joy out of you.
Suck the life out of you.
Drain your enthusiasm for living.

Don't get dragged into the whole
the-cross-is-not-enough-for-me-so-I-have -to-add-more-to-it HEX.

This book is about
hightailin' it out of Galatia County
to enjoy life with
God your FATHER.

You **CRAZY** Galatians!

Did someone put a **HEX** on you?

Have you taken leave of your senses?

Something **CRAZY** has happened,

for it's obvious that **YOU NO LONGER HAVE**

THE CRUCIFIED JESUS IN CLEAR FOCUS

in your lives. His sacrifice

on the cross was certainly set before

you clearly enough.

Galatians 3:1 (The Message Bible)

Read it again.
(S-L-O-W-L-Y...please!)

here
we
go

I.

How The Cross Disrupted Everything

*"For I decided to know nothing among you except Jesus Christ and him **CRUCIFIED**."*

1 Corinthians 2:2

BEFORE the cross   AFTER the cross

WAS   **IS**

what YOU did for God   what GOD did for you

The cross changed everything...
and still changes everything.

I was tryin' hard

I was trying hard to be a good Christian. Really.

But it seemed I was getting nowhere.

I was doing everything I was told I should do.

I was...
praying
reading my Bible
serving in church
avoiding most sins (at least the major ones)
sharing my faith when I got the opportunity
tithing and giving
fighting Satan

Then it dawned on me. Jews in the Old Testament under the Law of Moses had it easier than I did.

How did they get off so easy?
What did they have to do that was so tough?

The Jews had to take the day off on Saturday.
(No problem.)
They had to attend six feasts (parties) every year.
(Sounds good to me.)

*The next day he saw Jesus coming toward him, and said, "Behold, the **LAMB OF GOD**, who takes away the sin of the world!*

John 1:29

They could not eat bacon.
(Not happy about this one, but OK.)

And one more thing.

Every year they had to bring their best lamb to the high priest to have it sacrificed for their sins. Not just any lamb would do. This had to be a perfect lamb. You couldn't drag some lame, blind in one eye, sickly lamb to the high priest.

That's the way it worked. The only remedy for sin was the blood of innocent life. Innocent life had to be taken to pay for the sin. Nothing else would do.

And what could be more innocent than a small, cuddly lamb. So you had to bring a lamb to the priest. It had to be a perfect lamb because the priest was going to inspect it...carefully.

Guess what the priest did NOT do. He didn't inspect YOU. If your lamb was good then you were good to go.

He wouldn't say, "Well, your lamb looks great. Now let's talk about your prayer life and Bible reading plan."

Or "Your lamb is good, now how about your service in the temple? It looks like you have been slacking off a bit."

IF YOUR SACRIFICE WAS GOOD, YOU WERE GOOD. PERIOD.

Flash forward a few thousand years. It's still the same.

Today, we have a lamb.
A perfect lamb.
No spots.

*knowing that you were ransomed from the futile ways inherited from your forefathers, not with perishable things such as silver or gold, but with the **PRECIOUS BLOOD OF CHRIST**, like that of a **LAMB** without blemish or spot.*

1 Peter 1:18,19

No blemishes.
No sickness.
PERFECT.

His name is Jesus.

[God doesn't inspect you.
He inspects your sacrifice.]

Your sacrifice is Jesus, the Lamb of God.
You're good.

You can go now.

*Then they said to him, "What must we do, to be doing the **WORKS OF GOD**?" Jesus answered them, "This is the **WORK OF GOD**, that you **BELIEVE** in him whom he has sent."*

John 6:28-29

*But far be it from me to boast except in the **CROSS** of our Lord Jesus Christ,*

Galatians 6:14

so what day is it?

The Jews knew a special day was coming.

They referred to it in Psalm 112-118, known as the "Hallel." They recited it frequently at their celebrations and festivals.

They knew it as a mighty statement about God taking action on their behalf, the day He would BECOME their salvation.

It was the day a rejected stone would become the cornerstone.

But they did not know it referred to the crucifixion of the Messiah.

The day Jesus died on a cross.
The day He gave us His life.
The day He ended religion.
The day He BECAME our salvation.
The day...everything changed forever.

THAT is the day the Lord made.

I thank you that you have answered me and have **BECOME MY SALVATION.** *The stone that the builders rejected has become the* **CORNERSTONE.** *This is the LORD's doing; it is marvelous in our eyes.* **THIS IS THE DAY THAT THE LORD HAS MADE;** *let us rejoice and be glad in it.*

Psalm 118:21-24

Although it was a painful day for Jesus,
it is a happy day for us.

That was the day the crucifixion of Jesus became the cornerstone of our life.

Now THAT is a day you can rejoice in.
THAT is a day you can be glad about.

[You can't fully experience a relationship with
God until you grasp the significance of what
Jesus accomplished on the cross...THAT DAY.]

Because of THAT DAY...

You are free from paying for your own sins.
You are free from religious obligations.
You are made new.
You are secure in what God did for you.

And it's not because of what you did, or didn't do,
today,
or yesterday,
or the day before that.

And it is not about what you
promise to do tomorrow.

It is because of what happened on THAT DAY,
the day Jesus gave His life for you on the cross.

*let it be known
to all of you and
to all the people
of Israel that
by the name of
Jesus Christ of
Nazareth, whom
you **CRUCIFIED**,
whom God
raised from
the dead—by
him this man is
standing before
you well. This
Jesus is the
stone that was
rejected by you,
the builders,
which has
become the
CORNERSTONE.*

Acts 4:10-11

Christianity is not the sacrifice we make, but the sacrifice we trust.[1]

--P.T. Forsyth--

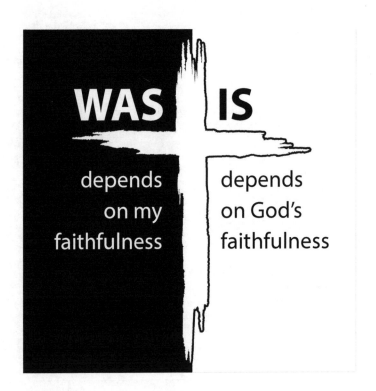

WAS — depends on my faithfulness

IS — depends on God's faithfulness

spray painting your new ferrari

I just bought you a brand new Ferrari 488 Spider.

3.9 liter.
8 cylinder turbo.
7 speed automatic transmission.
Red.
Cost: $272,700.

It's my GIFT to you. You're welcome.

Then I watch in horror as you do something unthinkable.
Unimagineable.
Crazy beyond words!

You take out a can of spray paint and declare, "It needs a little touch up right here," as you begin to spray red paint on the front hood.

I am mortified as I blurt out, "WHAT are you doing? This Ferrari does not need you to touch it up!" Right.

When Jesus had received the sour wine, he said, **"IT IS FINISHED,"** *and he bowed his head and gave up his spirit.*

John 19:30

And neither do you. Jesus did the work on the cross.

Your rescue is complete.
Your new life is complete.
Your acceptance by God is complete.
You are complete.

[
It is priceless.
It is paid off.
It is finished.
It is free to you.
]

You do NOT need to touch it up.
Put your religious spray paint away!

The last words Jesus spoke just before He died were these:

"It is finished."

He was not referring to His life. He resurrected three days later.

He used a business term in that day: "tetelestai."
It meant the account was paid in full.
It was a word that meant there is nothing left to pay.

So why are you still trying to complete your salvation?
Why are you trying to earn your way to Heaven?
Why are you trying to do stuff to make God like/accept/love you?

It is done. Over. Complete.

Jesus did NOT say...
It is almost done so you have to complete what I started by living right, keeping the rules, following Jesus, changing the world and whatever else your brand of Christianity tells you to do.

No. He said, "It is finished."

the day that killed religion

It was a day like no other.
It was the day the REVOLUTION began!

The sky went dark.
An earthquake shook the ground.
Dead folks came out of their tombs
and strolled around town.
The massive temple veil was
ripped in half from top to bottom.

It sounds like a sci-fi movie but it was real. It happened on the day Jesus was crucified. That was the day everything changed forever.

A rattled Roman soldier observed the strange occurrences surrounding the crucifixion and proclaimed, "This truly was the Son of God."

That was the day religion died.

(Everything changed...forever.)

Until then personal effort
to please God was the norm.
Religious ceremonies were required.
Sin loomed overhead.

And Jesus cried out again with a loud voice and yielded up his spirit.

*And behold, the curtain of the temple was **TORN IN TWO**, from top to bottom. And the **EARTH SHOOK**, and the **ROCKS WERE SPLIT**.*

*The tombs also were opened. And many bodies of the saints who had fallen asleep were **RAISED**, and coming **OUT OF THE TOMBS** after his resurrection they went into the holy city and appeared to many.*

God seemed distant.

After the crucifixion
Jesus resurrected from the dead.

Then the message of God's love and generosity
spread like wildfire.

Religion was over.
The rule-system was gone.

[**BUT...unfortunately...**
not everyone saw the obituary.]

(Shout "R.I.P.." to religion!)

Something BIG is happening.
This is a new day.

Jesus not only paid the full price for your sin,
He did something else.
Something amazing.

HE NAILED THE **OLD WAY** OF
RELIGIOUS DEMANDS TO THE CROSS.

The Roman soldiers thought they were only nailing
Jesus to the cross, but it turns out Jesus was doing
His own nailing. He nailed religion to the cross.

Not only did He die for your sins...
He killed the system that
condemned you.

He killed the old system of rules

When the

centurion and

those who

were with

him, keeping

watch over

Jesus, saw the

EARTHQUAKE

and what took

place, they

were filled with

AWE *and said,*

"TRULY THIS

WAS THE SON

OF GOD!"

Matthew 27:50-54

and regulations that obligated you.

You are free from religion.
There are no more to-do lists to reach God.

Jesus nailed religious
DEMANDS to the cross.

NO.
MORE.
DEMANDS.

(And don't pry out the nails!)

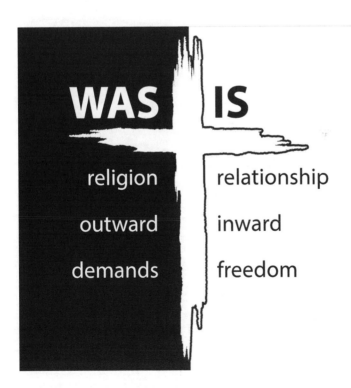

WAS IS

religion   relationship

outward   inward

demands   freedom

by
CANCELING
THE
RECORD
OF DEBT
that stood
against us
with its
LEGAL
DEMANDS.
This He
set aside,
NAILING
IT TO THE
CROSS.
Colossians 2:14

" *Jesus fired the Karma police with the cross.* **"**

Jeremiah Johnson
@gracepoint555

the big oops!

Oopsy. The devil made a little mistake.

If the devil and his gang had realized the power of the cross, they would never have had Jesus crucified.

Big mistake.

Because Jesus died for you,
God was able to
prepare great things for you.

[
Satan didn't expect the cross to
set you free,
pay for your sins,
connect you with God your Father.
]

He thought he was stopping Jesus.
He thought he was stopping God's plan.

Oops!

Instead, the cross ingnited God's plan to bring you into the amazing benefits of His family.

The devil NEVER saw that coming.

Surprise!

None of the rulers of this age understood this, for if they had, they **WOULD NOT HAVE CRUCIFIED** *the Lord of glory. But, as it is written,*

"What no eye has seen, nor ear heard, nor the heart of man imagined, what God has prepared for those who love him"

1 Corinthians 2:8,9

66

*The wages of
sin is death.
Jesus died.
Do the math
and celebrate.*

--Dr. Andrew Farley--
@drandrewfarley

99

it's a wonderful death

"It's a Wonderful Life" is a movie classic. The main character, George Bailey, is allowed to see what life would have been like for his family and hometown if he had never been born. I want to take an odd twist on that story.

Imagine what it would be like if Jesus had never been CRUCIFIED.

Imagine if:

Jesus came to Earth
Lived a perfect life
Told us about the Father and the Kingdom
Chose His disciples and sent them out,
But then just went back to Heaven without being
crucified – without being raised from the dead.

Imagine what that would be like.
Imagine trying to "live the Christian life"
if Jesus had NEVER been crucified.

Unfortunately, it is not hard to imagine at all.
It is not hard to imagine because that is the way we live.

We lose sight of the cross,
but still try to "live the Christian life."

*For the word of the **CROSS** is folly to those who are perishing, but to us who are being saved it is the **POWER OF GOD**.*

1 Corinthians 1:18

We do not live that way intentionally.
We do not realize we are living that way.

Living under the hex is when we try to do life with God
as if Jesus lived and taught,
but never died for us.

The great news in Bedford Falls and every other place is that Jesus Christ did not JUST:
come to Earth,
live a perfect life,
teach us about the Father and go back to Heaven.

[
He was also crucified for us.
He took our weakness and sin and shame to the cross.
He took the old way of religious effort to the cross.
]

Jesus Christ rose again and opened a NEW WAY of life with God!
Christ now lives in us.
On **THIS SIDE OF THE CROSS**,
He is our Christian life!

We do not live with God by rules and obligations on the outside.
That was nailed with Christ to the Cross.
NOW, CHRIST LIVES IN US.

Do not try to do life with God as if the cross never happened,
as if Jesus never died.
Do not lose sight of the Cross today.

It's a Wonderful Death!

FORGIVENESS

BC: God forgave you after you forgave others.
AC: He forgives you first so you can forgive others.

GOD'S PRESENCE

BC: It was about seeking God in the temple or through worship.
AC: Now about receiving presence of the Holy Spirit

GOD'S HOUSE

BC: Go to God's house
AC: Now we are God's house wherever we are.

PERSONAL REALITY

BC: Mere servant of God.
AC: Beloved son of God.

SPIRITUAL THIRST

BC: People thirsted for God.
AC: People are satisfied with living water flowing from within.

JUDGMENT

BC: God judges us.
AC: Jesus took our judgment.

GOD AS FATHER

BC: God was not known as Father.
AC: Jesus revealed God as caring Father.

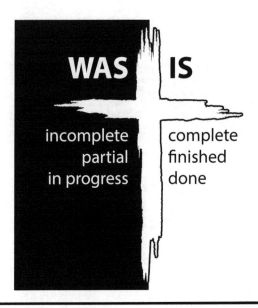

WAS | **IS**

incomplete | complete
partial | finished
in progress | done

have I been
a good boy?

The point of the Lord's Supper is to remind us to trust the crucifixion of Jesus. It is a time to examine our FAITH, not our behavior. It's a time to ask, "Am I trusting in what Jesus did for me on the cross?" It is not the time to ask, "Have I been a good boy?"

Read the ONLY time the disciples quoted
Jesus directly from the Gospels...

> ..."This is my body, which is for you. Do this in remembrance of me." In the same way also he took the cup, after supper, saying, "This cup is the new covenant in my **BLOOD.** Do this, as often as you drink it, in remembrance of me." For as often as you eat this bread and drink the cup, you **PROCLAIM THE LORD'S DEATH** until he comes.
> --Jesus (1 Corinthians 11:24-26)

our nike swoosh

The cross today has become the logo for Christianity. It's like the Nike swoosh for Christians.

For many, the cross is merely our trademark.

You can see a cross on top of church buildings.
Over Christian schools.
On necklaces.
On the cover of books.
On grave stones.
Crosses are everywhere.

The cross has become a symbol of religion.

(HOW IRONIC!)

Actually, it is the symbol of Jesus' crucifixion that **ENDED** religion and its merit-based approach to God.

For I decided to know **NOTHING** *among you except Jesus Christ and him* **CRUCIFIED.**

1 Corinthians 2:2

It's OK to wear a cross (no big deal).
Just realize it was never meant to be a religious symbol.

In reality, wearing a cross is a symbol...that you are NOT religious. (as it should be)

[NOTE: religious people killed Jesus.]

The cross ended the need for religion.

No longer do we need to strive to please God. Jesus pleased God for us.

[
Living on this side of the cross
means living with an understanding
of all that Jesus accomplished
for us in His crucifixion.
]

Now we can make a distinction between reality before the cross and reality after the cross.

It is no wonder Paul said the cross was his message.

We live in the joy and freedom of knowing that what Jesus did for us is all we need. We experience the transforming power of grace.

The cross means you are DONE with religion. (now breathe!)

but we preach Christ ***CRUCIFIED,*** *a stumbling block to Jews and folly to Gentiles,*

1 Corinthians 1:23

yoa head all jam up?

In case you're wondering how the
Pidgin Bible Translates Galatians 3:1-5
(we know you are)

You guys from Galatia, yoa head all jam up! Befo time we wen tell you guys **strait out da Good Stuff** bout how odda guys wen kill Jesus Christ on top da cross an he wen mahke fo us. But now you guys no lissen to da true stuff. Somebody wen **put kahuna on top you guys,** o wat? Ony one ting I like you guys tell me: How you guys wen get God's Spirit? Cuz you guys wen do wat da Rules say? O cuz you guys wen trus da Good Stuff From God dat you guys wen hear? Fo shua, cuz you guys wen **trus da Good Stuff From God!** You guys not tinking, o wat? You guys wen trus God's Spirit in da beginning. **But now in da end you guys goin try fo do everyting wit yoa own power?** All da stuff dat wen happen to you guys -- fo notting? O good fo someting? God stay give you guys his Spirit, an he do awesome stuff fo you guys wit his power. **You tink he do um cuz you guys do wat da Rules say, o cuz you guys trus da stuff you guys wen hear?**

Galatians 3:1-5
Pidgin Bible Translation by the Pidgin Bible Translation Group
(actual translation from a Hawaiian dialect)

snake on a stick

Jesus pointed to one
--and only one--
Old Testament story to explain His crucifixion.
ONE story.

(And it was a strange story.)

The Jewish people were suffering
from snake bites that were killing them.

God told Moses to make a bronze snake
and lift it up on a pole.
Moses did it.
When the people LOOKED at the snake
lifted up on the pole,
they were cured.

(BOOM)
Cured.

That's all they did: LOOK.

Simply looking at the uplifted snake cured them.
Think about that.
All they did was...look.

*And as Moses lifted up the serpent in the wilderness, so must the Son of Man be **LIFTED UP**, that whoever believes in him may have eternal life.*

John 3:14-15

They didn't fast,
pray hard,
attend meetings
or memorize scripture.
They looked at the bronze snake.

That's all.

Jesus said He was like that bronze snake.

He said He would be lifted up.
That was a term He used to refer
to His upcoming crucifixion.

In the same way, looking at Jesus' crucifixion is the CURE for sin.

Among other things,
sin is a spiritual disease.
It needs a cure.

The cross cures us of sin.

Stop working to earn your
salvation/redemption/forgiveness.

Fixate on the truth that Jesus died for YOU on the cross.

Just look.
Soooooo simple.

*He himself bore our sins in his body on the **TREE**, that we might die to sin and live to righteousness. By his wounds you have been **HEALED**.*

1 Peter 2:24

My sin—
oh, the bliss of this glorious thought!
My sin, not in part but the whole,
Is nailed to the cross,
and I bear it no more,
Praise the Lord,
praise the Lord,
O my soul!

from "It Is Well With My Soul"
Horatio G. Spafford
1873

*In speaking of a **NEW** covenant,*
*he makes the first one **OBSOLETE**.*
*And what is becoming **OBSOLETE** and*
***GROWING OLD** is ready to **VANISH AWAY**.*

Hebrews 8:13

timing is everything

Jesus died and left you an inheritance.

You can't get an inheritance until somebody dies and leaves you something. That's the way it works.

Death first. Then inheritance.

That's why the inheritance Jesus left to us did not take effect until AFTER He died.

[It was NOT in effect in the Old Testament.
It was NOT even in effect when
Jesus roamed around in the Gospels.]

Keep that in mind when you read the Gospels or the Old Testament.

There was no inheritance until Jesus died. That's when it started.

But now
by faith in Him,
you have an inheritance.
A big one.

an
INHERITANCE
*that is
imperishable,
undefiled, and
unfading, kept in
heaven for you,*

1 Peter 1:4

*For a will takes
effect only at*
DEATH,
*since it is not
in force as long
as the one who
made it is alive.*

Hebrews 9:17

OLD	NEW
deadly religion	vibrant relationship
rule-keeping	trust
doing stuff for God	God doing stuff through you
effort	rest
guilt	peace
shame	acceptance
fear	peace
God loves everybody in general	God is wild about YOU individually
hard	easy
God is mad at you	God is mad about you
press into God	God always with me
obligation	freedom

all inclusive guilt trip

Do not let anyone use
the parting words of Jesus
to lay a guilt trip on you.

[
The passage, commonly known as
"the great commission", is used (misused),
as much as any other passage today,
to guilt God's children into action.
]

It is a modern day example of the hex.
The speech goes something like this:

**Jesus said ALL authority
has been given to Him.**
(You better do what He says
or you are in big trouble).
It was the LAST words of Jesus.
(Don't you dare disobey His LAST words).
Jesus COMMANDED us to make disciples.
(It's the law, buddy,
and not just a suggestion).
**If you do NOT have a group of disciples
around you, SHAME on you!**
(Wipe that smile off your guilty face).

*And Jesus
came and
said to
them, "All
authority
in heaven
and on
earth has
been given
to me. Go
therefore
and make
disciples
of all
nations,...*

Matthew 28:18-19

That is pretty much how it goes.

Add some music in the background and/or the right voice inflections, and you have just effectively unloaded a boatload of guilt on an entire congregation. They will feel an enormous weight of obligation. 99% of them will not change how they live, but now they will at least feel condemned about not doing enough. The 1% may try to do something in their own effort for a while so they will not feel so guilty.

It is full-blown hex mode.

If the task of making disciples is THE ONE, BIG thing we are supposed to be focusing on, why is it never mentioned in any of the letters to the believers?

[We never see Paul or Peter or John
quoting the words of Jesus
about making disciples.]

What DID the letters to the earliest believers deal with? Among other things, they did talk much about getting along with ONE ANOTHER in the Body of Christ.

That reminds us of something else Jesus said about being disciples. He said His new commandment was for us to love each other the way He loves us.

Then, he said the way the world will know we are connected to Him is by our love for each other.

When we turn the "great commission" into the "great guilt trip", we get off track.

We contradict the rest of what the New Testament says about grace. We use law to motivate instead of trusting the Spirit.

We cause others to lose sight of the Father's affection for them. We encourage dead works.

Sadly, we put the hex on people.

When Jesus prayed for us the night before He died, He did not pray that we would all go out and "make disciples." His prayer for us was that we would all be one. He said that our oneness in Him and in the Father would lead the world to believe that Jesus was sent from God.

Jesus did not intend for his words to the eleven to be used as a guilt trip.

As we experience the reality of the crucified and risen Christ in our lives, it is normal/good/fantastic to tell others about what He has done.

However...

If you NEVER lead someone else to Jesus, it's OK. Don't feel guilty/condemned. You still belong to God through Jesus. You do NOT have to share your faith to be acceptable to God.

"

Religion says, "make every effort to work perfectly." God says, "make every effort to rest in My perfect work."

Nathan Houtsma
@nathanhoutsma

do the math

Sometimes it's helpful to know if something is emphasized in the New Testament writings. So here's a breakdown.

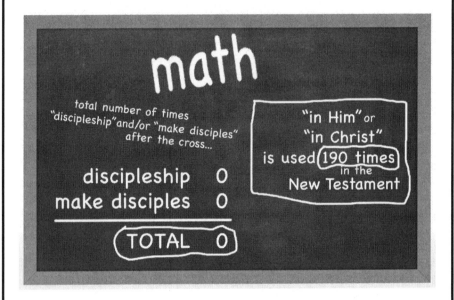

Paul the Apostle never mentioned discipleship in the New Testament. (HINT: every believer in Acts was called a disciple.)

He never even told anyone to "follow" Christ. That was never his emphasis. He simply told people to put their faith in Jesus, to trust Him. Then he explained that they were IN CHRIST.

HERE'S THE POINT! Your personal reality IN CHRIST is more important than the stuff you do for God.

So how are you doing spiritually?

If you are IN CHRIST then you are doing well because Jesus is doing very well spiritually.

how rules backfire

If you want to cause someone to be more likely to sin, I know exactly how to do it. If you want someone to be overwhelmed by a wrong desire, there is an easy way to make it happen.

The Bible tells us how.

The answer? Make a rule against it.

One sure-fire way to make the urge to sin stronger is to make a law that commands you NOT to do it.

The New Testament says that "the law gives sin it's power."

It says, "For apart from the law, sin lies dead."

It says that our sinful passions are "aroused by the law."

(Wow! Think about that!)

*For sin is the sting that results in death, and the **LAW** gives sin its **POWER**.*

1 Corinthians 15:56 (NLT)

*For when we were in the realm of the flesh, the sinful passions **AROUSED BY THE LAW** were at work in us*

Romans 7:5

Not only do rules not keep us from doing wrong, they actually CAUSE us to do wrong. When you know you are not supposed to do something, you want to do it even more.

Laws and rules make sin stronger!

Many people are afraid of grace because they think it promotes sin. Actually, the opposite is true. Sin is definitely destructive, but every well-intended system of rules eventually increases sin.

[Rules and laws do NOTHING
to change someone's heart.
ABSOLUTELY NOTHING.]

At the very best, rules can force some outward behavior for a little while as the heart grows cold. When we say God's grace is free, but then also try to depend on obligation to rules, we are living under the hex.

When we realize that God is not putting us under obligation, the power of sin is dissolved.

When we get out from underneath rules and threat of punishment, the desire to rebel starts to fade.

[It is the LOVE and GRACE of God through
His Spirit that transforms the human heart
from the INSIDE.]

THAT is good news!

But sin, seizing an opportunity through the commandment, ***PRODUCED*** *in me all kinds of covetousness. For apart from the law, sin lies dead.*

Romans 7:8

The ultimate freedom is in knowing the love of God. The ultimate bondage is in trying to earn it.

Dr. Eric Skidmore
@gracectrhouston

hamster wheelin' it

At 6 years old I got my first real pet, a hamster. I named him (or her, not sure which) "Brownie." Brownie lived in a standard sized hamster cage with a water dispenser, and food cup and a metal wheel. For some unknown reason Brownie ran on that wheel for hours at a time, normally all night long.

Maybe he needed the exercise, but I don't think so. I took him out of the cage and played with him plenty. And since the wheel was fastened to the cage he certainly didn't go anywhere.

So what was the point to all that activity?

I'm certainly glad we Christians don't do anything like that. You won't catch us engaged in pointless activity.

Hmmm.

I'm not so sure.

Recently, I was listening to a group discuss their walk with Christ. They explained how they earnestly desired to live a life pleasing to God. They were all striving to figure out what areas of their lives needed

the most work.
They were self-focused to the max.
They constantly asked the question of each other,
"How is your walk with the Lord doing?"
They put every area of their lives under the microscope.

Psalm 139:23-24 was the scripture they most often appealed to?

These are great verses...
IF you were Jewish and lived under the Law of Moses.
IF you lived before Jesus died and gave you His own righteousness.

[
Today, however, thanks to Jesus and what He did for us,
you do NOT have to spend your days asking God
to dig up every failure in your life.
]

You can get off that hamster wheel.

It's not going anywhere anyway.
Five...ten...twenty years from now
you will still be praying the same prayer.

And who wants to hang out with a God who focuses on scrutinizing your every weakness, failure and sin? Most of us avoid people like that.

[
Do we really think Jesus came to earth, died for us
and rose again so we could spend our lives
stressing over every weakness?
]

Live on THIS SIDE of the cross.

Accept His forgiveness, grace and love.

And relax.

all 'bout me

Religion is all about me.

It's about what I do and don't do.
It sounds like it's about God but not so much.

Religion is all about my obligations...

MY church attendance
MY righteousness
MY Bible reading plan
MY prayer life
MY virtues/values
MY goodness
MY obedience
MY efforts
MY service

Faith, real faith, is all about Jesus.

It's about who He is,
what He did,
what He does.
He's the Savior.
Not me.
Or you.
It's about Him, Jesus.

(You got this! Right?)

Are you tired? Worn out?

BURNED OUT ON RELIGION?

Come to me. Get away with me and you'll recover your life. I'll show you how to take a real rest. Walk with me and work with me— watch how I do it. Learn the **UNFORCED RHYTHMS OF GRACE**. I won't lay anything heavy or ill-fitting on you. Keep company with me and you'll learn to live freely and lightly. --Jesus

Matthew 11:28-30
(MSG)

spitting on the sabbath

Jesus was NOT religious.

Jesus was constantly at odds with the religious leaders of His day. He was attacked because He wasn't religious enough for them.

Jesus broke their religious rules. He criticized the religious leaders. Constantly.

He hung around people
who didn't meet their approval.

He made statements that
violated their religious doctrine.

Jesus disrupted religion. (BIG TIME)

The Jewish leaders didn't plot to execute Jesus because He talked about love. They plotted against Him because He disrupted everything religious. They even accused Jesus of being possessed by a demon.

Religion is about imposing rules on people to gain God's favor. Jesus brought a message about God's

When the Pharisees saw this, they asked his disciples, "Why does your teacher (Jesus) eat with tax collectors and sinners?"

Matthew 9:11

favor already being available through His grace.

Because religion is devoid of life, it has to fill the void with symbols,
rules,
decor,
pageantry.

The life that Jesus gives is real and authentic.
It does NOT need all of that.

Religion is NOT alive.
It is empty and fake.

You do NOT have to be religious to receive what Jesus did for you. You just have to be a little humble.

Just realize your need for a Savior.
Trust Him.

That's all. He'll do the rest.
Is it that simple?
(Yep.)

It's about relationship, not religion. Love, not rules.

Apparently some traditions
need to be broken.

Jesus once healed a blind man by spitting. That's right, with SPIT!

Having said these things, he **SPIT ON THE GROUND** *and made mud with the saliva. Then he anointed the man's eyes with the mud and said to him, "Go, wash in the pool of Siloam" So he went and washed and came back seeing.*

John 9:6-7

A blind man comes to Jesus and wants to be healed. Jesus spits on the ground, makes some mud and wipes it on the man's eyes. He then tells the man something he would not have had to tell me, "Go wash that off." This is what the Bible says Jesus did. It worked. The man was healed. Now the question. Why?

Why did Jesus need to spit to get the man healed?
Was that really necessary?
He could have just touched the man's eyes.
Or spoke over him.
Why spit?

[It turns out the Pharisees
  had a real problem with
  spitting on the Sabbath.]

Now it was a Sabbath day when Jesus made the mud and opened his eyes.

Jesus purposely tweaked the religious power brokers.

He violated the Pharisees' rules about the Sabbath.
Jesus ruthlessly confronted the stuffy religious people who cared more about their rules than about people.

Jesus was more about people than religious traditions.

Go ahead.
Don't be afraid.
Spit on the Sabbath.

66

When I tell you that Jesus hung out with sinners and you respond with **"I need to do more of that,"** *then you do not know who you are in that story.*

unknown

99

this is your crummy, miserable life

I was taught in church growing up that one day I would stand before God and He would replay my entire life on a massive, high-resolution screen. I would stand there as the whole world would watch every good/bad deed I ever did. At the conclusion of my life story God would make a determination as to whether I made it into Heaven or not.

My only chance was that my good deeds would outweigh my bad deeds.

If that is the way it works then
WHAT IS THE POINT IN HAVING A SAVIOR?

Jesus is your Savior.
You will NOT be judged.
He took your judgment.
You were found guilty and He took the penalty.
That's what He did for you on the cross.
It's done.

Since you PASSED from death to life
you will not be judged.

In Revelation 20:12 only the DEAD get judged!

HINT: Since Jesus made you alive, you're not dead anymore.
This judgment is NOT for you.

You're alive in Him...forever.

If your name is in the BOOK,
you will not be judged by the BOOKS.
(The books record every action,
good and bad, of the spiritually dead.)

But the only book that matters is the Book of Life.

If your name is in the Book of Life, you are good.
Jesus took your judgment.
There is no judgment
left for you to take.

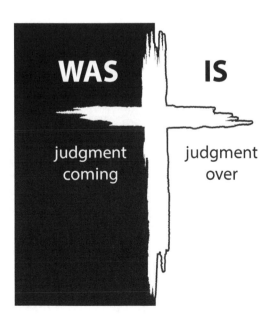

WAS

IS

judgment
coming

judgment
over

And I saw the dead, great and small, standing before the throne, and books were opened. Then another book was opened, which is the **BOOK OF LIFE.** *And the* **DEAD** *were judged by what was written in the* **BOOKS,** *according to what they had done.*

Revelation 20:12

whack-a-mole religion

Many live in whack-a-mole religion.

We get obsessed with sin
and neglect relationship with Jesus.

Conquering sin.
Avoiding sin.
Preaching about sin.
Identifying sin.
Confessing sin.
Repenting of sin.

We spent our effort focused on
tamping down sin.
Anytime a sin would raise its ugly head
--which is quite often--
we would work to smash it back down.

I understand that.
I am totally against sin.
Sin is bad.
No question.

The problem is that the whack-a-mole technique is never-ending.
No matter how many times we attempted to knock a sin back down
it would always come back. Always.

Just about the time we were able to knock selfishness back into its hole, unforgiveness would pop up. Then by the time we knocked unforgiveness back into its hole, bitterness and lust would pop up.
It was a never ending cycle of failure. **But worst of all it would take our focus off of the love and acceptance of our Father God.**

What started as a relationship with Jesus unraveled into a system of INDEPENDENT effort, frustration and futility. That is not the life Jesus carved out for you when He died, resurrected and gave you His life.

There is a better way.

A Jesus-focused life produces freedom.
A sin-focused life produces frustration.

A Jesus-focused life produces good results.
A sin-focused life produces...more sin.

Living on this side of the cross means daily
trusting in the life that Jesus lives in you and through you.

Let Him whack the moles.
He's better at it.

hot grace, cold self

What do you get when you mix hot with cold?

Lukewarm.

(NOT GOOD.)

I like hot tea.
I like cold tea.
Lukewarm tea? No thanks!
Room temperature tea? YUCK!

In the book of Revelation, Jesus brings this up to a church in a town called "Laodicea." He lets them know that He is upset with them for being "lukewarm." He comes down hard on them.

But what does it mean to be "lukewarm?"

I was taught that "lukewarm" meant I wasn't working hard enough to serve the Lord. I got the impression I needed to do more for God to keep from being lukewarm.

Try harder!
Do more!
(SMOKIN' HOT YIKES!)

Jesus does NOT tell them to:
work harder,
be better disciples,
or obey more commandments.
They didn't need more effort.

It turns out that the lukewarm people in Laodicea were a bit self-absorbed. They thought they had come to the point where they didn't need Jesus.

[They were so confident in their own ability and accomplishments that they left Jesus standing outside of His own church. Picture that.]

Jesus pointed out that they were NOT rich. In fact, He tells them they are pitiful, poor, blind and naked. They just didn't know it. They felt like they were doing just fine on their own.

That's what religion does.

Religion blinds you to your own need for Jesus and leaves you consumed with your own ability. Then Jesus gets locked outside.

In reality, they were doing the same thing the folks in Galatia were doing, mixing God's grace with their own efforts.

[God's grace is red hot.
Self-sufficiency is stone cold.
Mix the two and you have lukewarm.]

Jesus NEVER asked them to work harder. He just wanted them to open the door so He could come in and have dinner.

He just wanted to hang out with them.

and the shame of your nakedness may not be seen, and salve to anoint your eyes, so that you may see. Those whom I love, I reprove and discipline, so be zealous and repent. ***BEHOLD, I STAND AT THE DOOR AND KNOCK.*** *If anyone hears my voice and opens the door, I will come in to him and eat with him, and he with me.*

Revelation 3:16-20

saved by grace

martha gone wild

We have made this so-called "Christian life" thing WAY...too...complicated.

This is illustrated by the story of what happened one day when Jesus visited the home of Mary and Martha. Martha was busy and bothered with many things, but Mary sat at the feet of Jesus listening to His word.

Both knew Jesus.
Both were sincere.
Martha made it complicated.
Mary kept it simple.

[Martha is an illustration of the way things were on the other side of the cross.]

She was focused on all the things that SHE NEEDED TO DO.

Mary simply "heard His word." Martha was distracted by many things, but Jesus said that Mary had chosen the good part, the one thing that was needed. We "hear" the Spirit of God in our spirit.

And she had a sister called Mary, who sat at the Lord's feet and listened to his teaching. But Martha was ***DISTRACTED WITH MUCH SERVING****.*

Luke 10:39-40

Walking with God is simply hearing His voice within and responding to Him.

Paul told the believers at Corinth that he was concerned that their minds were being corrupted from the SIMPLICITY in Christ. He compared it to how Eve was deceived by the serpent in the Garden of Eden.

Walking with God is simple.

While Scripture is inspired by God, LIFE IN CHRIST IS A RELATIONSHIP WITH A REAL PERSON, NOT WITH A BOOK.

You can trust Him to lead. You can trust in His Spirit to teach you. You can trust in Him to bring you back on course like a GPS when you take a wrong turn.

Sadly, when someone first comes to know Christ, we have a tendency to load them up with a mountain of expectations and obligations and information. Intentional or not, we do them NO FAVOR when we get new believers to be more in tune with our voice than with the voice of their shepherd.

Jesus is the shepherd. He is the shepherd who can both rescue His sheep AND then lead them.

The best thing we can do for a new believer is simply to encourage them to listen to the voice of the One who drew them in the first place.

Yes, more experienced brothers and sisters can help others sort out the daily walk and help a new believer recognize the voice of Jesus.

The problem comes when a so-called "leader" tries to REPLACE the voice of the Spirit in someone's life with THE LEADER'S VOICE.

ON THIS SIDE OF THE CROSS, it is really not that complicated.

[
Trust the One who is your life.
Trust the One who lives within you.
Trust the One who loves you more than you know.
]

He will lead you. He will.

you don't owe God nuttin'

Heresy!

How can I say we do NOT owe God anything?
Am I crazy?
Don't I know who God is?
And what He did for me?

Ask the average believer if they owe God anything and they will look at you like you are crazy. Who, in their right theological mind, would suggest we do not owe God anything? Well…the apostle Paul for one. He said that God cancelled the record of debt that stood against us with its legal demands.

If the record of debt has been cancelled by God, that means you…do…not…OWE…God… anything! (STUNNING!)

If you believe you owe God anything, it means you do not really believe that He cancelled the debt on the cross. Did the death of Jesus on the cross cancel your debt or didn't it?

"Yeah, but isn't God worthy of all glory?" Yes.
"But isn't God our Creator and Savior?" Yes.

"But isn't God deserving of complete submission?" Yes.
"Then, don't we owe Him everything?" No. No. No.

God Himself cancelled the record of debt that was against us. You
cannot believe, on the one hand, that Jesus paid your debt in full on
the cross, and also believe that you owe God something. If we owe God
anything, then Jesus did not pay our debt in full.

Way too many preachers try to pile the debt onto the backs of believers
to make them feel guilty about not doing enough for God. THAT, my
friends, is a denial of the work of Christ on the Cross.

When I realize that Jesus paid
ALL of my debt on the cross,
When I realize that God
cancelled the debt once and for all,
When I realize that I do not owe God anything,
All of a sudden,
I realize how fantastic God is!

No one likes to hang around someone
when you owe them something.
Nothing ruins a family reunion
like borrowing money from your relatives.

No wonder your Cousin Eddie gets nervous at Thanksgiving,
then leaves early.

[
We tend to avoid our creditors. If you do not feel endeared to God,
maybe it is because you still think you are in debt to Him.
]

It is no wonder that many people do not want to do life with God. They
have been told they owe Him everything. They do not realize that, on
THIS SIDE OF THE CROSS, the debt has been cancelled.

That is great news!

God longs for you to know how much he loves you.
He wants you to do life with Him because you actually want to do so, not because you are making a payment on a huge debt.

He wants you to know that
you do not owe Him anything.
Look at the cross.
The debt has been paid.

III.

How God Made You New

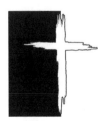

*Therefore, if anyone is in Christ, he is a **NEW CREATION**. The old has passed away; behold, the new has come.*

2 Corinthians 5:17

WAS

IS

striving
to
become

believing
who
you are
in Christ

Faith in Jesus and His crucifixion doesn't merely improve us...but makes us new.

kickball

In my elementary school kickball was king. And I was a horrible kickball player.

The game is simple enough: someone rolls the ball in your direction, you kick it as hard as you can and then run like you're on fire to first base. You try to get there before some other kid grabs the ball and hurls it at you.

Before the game started, two captains chose kids one by one to be on their team. The problem with that was my past performance in kickball was less than impressive. Therefore, the captains regularly--and reluctantly-chose me last or close to it.

That's not a great feeling.

Obviously, neither captain was pumped about picking me for their team. So even after I finally got picked, it was an afterthought, not something that the captains planned. "OK, I'll take Roger," was what I heard most days.

Thankfully, God is not a kickball captain looking for the best players.

He is a Father.
Your DAD.

He ***CHOSE*** *us in him before the foundation of the world,*

Ephesians 1:4

He picked YOU.

Not because of what you can do for Him.

Don't let the doctrinal ramifications rob you.
Don't get bogged down with trying to unravel the
time line. You don't have to understand all the details
to accept the fact that God chose you.

He picked you because
He wanted YOU.
Not reluctantly.
Not by accident.
On purpose.
He chose you.
Yes, YOU.

(Let that sink in.)

don't let this go to your head, but...

Jesus said that John the Baptist was greater than anyone born up until that time.

Wow! That means Johnny B was the superstar of the Bible before the cross. (Of course, not counting Jesus) That means he ranked above Abraham, Moses, King David, Elijah and the rest of the Biblical heroes. That's quite an endorsement coming from Jesus.

But here's the kicker.

Jesus said one more thing.
He said there is someone even greater than Johnny B.
Wanna guess who?
YOU.

How is that possible?

Jesus said that anyone--even the least---in the Kingdom of Heaven (any believer) is greater than John the Baptist!

THAT IS AMAZING!

*Truly, I say to you, among those born of women there has arisen no one **GREATER** than John the Baptist. Yet the one who is least in the kingdom of heaven is **GREATER** than he.*

Matthew- 11:11

Did you catch THAT?

(REWIND THAT AND PLAY IT AGAIN)

Jesus said the least of believers in the Kingdom on this side of the cross is greater than John the Baptist who lived before the cross.

Soooooo.

Even if you do not FEEL strong,
Even if you do not FEEL spiritual,
Jesus says you are greater than any of those giant-killing, sea-splitting, ark-building, furnace-defying, lion-stopping hot shots.

Whoa! (Remember, do NOT let this go to your head.)

In Christ you are greater than anyone who lived before the cross.

Through Christ living in us, we have what those old dudes before the cross could only dream of.

Today, as members of the Body of Christ, you and I have more going for us than any of those who lived before the Cross.

Don't sell yourself short.
The God who created the universe says
He has placed the life of His Son inside you.
You and Christ are now one.
You are in Him and He is in you.
That is who you are!

Don't let this to go to your head (in an arrogant way)...
but DO let it go to your heart.

WAS | IS

1 Have mercy on me, O God,
according to your steadfast love;
according to your abundant mercy
blot out my transgressions.
2 Wash me thoroughly from my iniquity,
and cleanse me from my sin!
3 For I know my transgressions,
and my sin is ever before me.
4 Against you, you only, have I sinned
and done what is evil in your sight,
so that you may be justified
in your words
and blameless in your judgment.
5 Behold, I was brought forth in iniquity,
and in sin did my mother conceive me.
6 Behold, you delight in truth
in the inward being,
and you teach me wisdom
in the secret heart.
7 Purge me with hyssop,
and I shall be clean;
wash me, and I shall be
whiter than snow.
8 Let me hear joy and gladness;
let the bones that you
have broken rejoice.
9 Hide your face from my sins,
and blot out all my iniquities.
10 Create in me a clean heart, O God,
and renew a right spirit within me.
11 Cast me not away from your presence,
and take not your Holy Spirit from me.
12 Restore to me the joy
of your salvation,
and uphold me with a willing spirit.

(from Psalm 51)

In Christ,
God has
already
done
all of this
for you.

You do
not need
to keep
asking.

Sounds like
good news
to me.
(woohoo!!!)

the doctor will see you now

On Sept. 10, 2001, our dad had major surgery.

It was to diagnose and, hopefully, to remove the mass that had shown up in the MRI. With a range of possible outcomes, I will never forget the sense of relief and joy we experienced when one of the surgeons came into the waiting room, smiling, to tell us the news.

THERE WAS NO CANCER!
We took him at his word and thanked God.

My brother and I had not seen what was in his abdomen. Even if we had, we would not have known how to diagnose it. However, because an experienced surgical oncologist gave us a good report, we immediately knew the truth about Dad's condition.

We took the surgeon at his word. Dad was on his way to getting better. God gave us another wonderful 13 years with him.

Just as we depend on a doctor to diagnose our physical condition, we can depend on God, the Great Physician, to diagnose our true spiritual condition.

God has done the MRI on you.
The spiritual blood work and surgery is complete.
He sees what you cannot see and He has a great report.
Because of what God in Christ did for you on the cross,
you have been made completely new!

God's Spirit now lives in you.
You have a new personal reality.
On the inside, you have been joined with Christ.

You may not feel like it or act like it at times,
but that is who God says you are!
The truest thing about you is what God says about you.
His testimony is the final word.
In your spirit, you are one with Christ.
Believe Him.

He is not just saying that to make you feel better.
It really is true.

It is ours to believe as God reveals this
incredible good news to your heart through His Spirit.

QUIT TRYING TO BECOME
WHO YOU ALREADY ARE!

ON THIS SIDE OF THE CROSS,
your reliable test result from
the Great Physician is fantastic news.

the idol of spiritual growth

"Now wait just a cotton-pickin' minute.
Every Christian knows that
growth is the ultimate goal!"

HOW CAN SPIRITUAL GROWTH POSSIBLY BE AN IDOL?

When I was growing up, I was anxious to grow taller.
Like many kids, I would stand against the back of my
bedroom door and have someone mark the door
at the top of my head. A few months later, I would
repeat the process to see if I could place a new mark a
little higher.

We often do something similar with our spiritual
height. While my preoccupation with my physical
height only lasted maybe 6 or 8 years, I was
preoccupied with my spiritual height for many more
years.

I desperately wanted to grow spiritually.
I wanted to be able to overcome temptation.
I wanted to have insights into Scripture.
I wanted to experience the power of the Holy Spirit.

Like a little boy putting marks on the back of the
bedroom door, I was constantly trying to measure
my spiritual height. I would get frustrated when my
spiritual growth seemed to flat-line or even worse,

back up an inch or two. Looking back,
I was making spiritual growth an idol.

I was focused more on ME and MY performance than I was on JESUS CHRIST and HIS performance.

Jesus encouraged his listeners not to worry about physical needs and physical growth. He reminds them that their heavenly Father takes care of feeding the birds and clothing the wild flowers. Anxiety over our physical well-being happens when we do not realize that we have a heavenly Father who loves us more than we know.

The same is true spiritually.

Much of my desire to be spiritually mature was really coming from not knowing how much God had already done for me.

When we know we are already completely loved by our heavenly Father, we are free from trying to perform for Him. We are free to enjoy the relationship with Him.

I cannot make myself grow spiritually any more than I could make myself grow physically.

Where there is life, there is growth.

As we quit worrying about growing spiritually and as we recognize God's love for us, a funny thing happens.
We start to grow...in grace.

On this side of the cross, we can stop measuring ourselves on the back of the spiritual bedroom door.

We can trust Him to bring about the growth in His time.

you are here*

It is fairly common for praise and worship songs to focus on coming into God's presence. They are written and sung as if something still needs to happen to bring us into God's presence.

Too often, they largely ignore the fantastic reality of God's presence that we have--here and now--on this side of the cross.

The good news in Jesus Christ is that we no longer have to strive to come into God's presence! He lives in us through His Spirit all the time!

The notion of coming into God's presence through praise music or prayer or Scripture is what life was like BEFORE the cross.

Jesus promised that when His Spirit would come, we would be in Him and He would be in us. You cannot get any closer than that.

I cannot "come into His presence" any more than I can come into the presence of my own physical heart.

We are the Body of Christ.
We are God's temple.
Christ lives in us.

I am not always conscious of Christ in me just as I am not always conscious of my beating heart. So, it is helpful to be reminded who we already are in Christ and who He is in us. That is different, though, than needing to come into His presence.

Jesus Himself demonstrated this.
Did He ever "come into the Father's presence"? No.
He and the Father were one.

He, at times, went away from the crowds to enjoy the undistracted company of the Father, but He never left the Father's presence. He couldn't! The Father and Jesus were one.

In the same way,
Jesus and the believer are one today.
It is fantastic to know that Christ and you are one.
He lives in you.

ON THIS SIDE OF THE CROSS,
you do not need to
"come into His presence."

He will never leave you nor forsake you.
Nothing you can do will separate you
from the love of God that is in Jesus Christ.

He is our constant location.

[HINT: You never have to pray, "God, be with me."]

I have been crucified with Christ. It is **NO LONGER I WHO LIVE,** *but* **CHRIST WHO LIVES IN ME.** *And the life I now live in the flesh I live by faith in the Son of God, who loved me and gave himself for me.*

Galatians 2:20

i quit trying to live the christian life

Author Wayne Jacobsen tells the true story about a teenage girl who returned home after attending a Christian youth meeting. When asked by her parents what they talked about, she replied,

"Same ol', same ol'. You know, God's good. You're bad. Try harder." [1]

For many of us, that sums up how we are trying to live what many call, "the Christian life."

Looking back, I often tried to perform for God so that He and I would both feel good about how I was doing. I wanted God to be pleased with me. So, the way to get there was to try harder. At least that is what it seemed like.

I became more and more frustrated trying to "live the Christian life."

The harder I tried, the weaker I felt.
I knew I was still God's child and forgiven.
I just did not feel very spiritual.

Intellectually, I knew God loved me,
but I felt He was disappointed in me.

I would say it is all by grace,
but God still seemed rather demanding and hard to please.

He was good, but it sure seemed like I was bad.
And TRYING HARDER WAS NOT WORKING.

God is patient.

Somewhere along the way I began to see that "living the Christian life" is not just difficult. It...is...impossible.

All the time my heavenly Father was helping me see that He was
not asking me to live the Christian life. He was waiting to live His life
through me.

The difference is NOT just semantics.
Real life comes from the inside.
God is not asking you to live the Christian life.
He loves you and is asking you to trust Him to live His life through you.

Don't worry about the end result. That will take care of itself in time. He will be your "Christian Life." Relax and expect His Life in you to grow over time and displace the old tendencies.

captivated by Jesus

The problem of the Galatian believers was that their focus strayed off of Jesus Christ and His completed work on the cross. They started well, but were trying to finish by helping God through their own effort.

Day to day, they were no longer CAPTIVATED by Jesus Christ.

The method of the enemy is to get us captivated by any other "good" thing or person or effort instead of by Jesus Christ and His work.

There are many "good" things that can help direct us to Jesus Christ. The problem comes when we allow those things to become more prominent in our lives than Jesus Himself. Those things or people or ideas become a poor substitute for Jesus.

We start to trust in them more than in the living Savior. In this way, they end up replacing Christ in our lives.

Many genuine believers have a half-baked view of all that Jesus Christ won for us. As a result, we try to carry on through human effort what can only be finished through the miracle of Christ living in us.

Focus on Jesus Christ and the incredible work that He did for you.

Freedom comes from being captivated ONLY by Him!

**BE CAREFUL ABOUT
BEING CAPTIVATED BY...**

**Any set of principles.
Any teacher/author/minister.
Any style of praise music.
Any Sunday morning gathering.
Bible study groups/series.
Ministry activities/programs.**

There is NO...
program/author/principle/
conference/song/teacher/video/
doctrine/liturgy/ministry
that died for you.

None.

I am truly captivated
only by Jesus Christ...
the One who actually did
die for me.

*But I am afraid that as the serpent deceived Eve by his cunning, your thoughts will be led astray from a sincere and **PURE DEVOTION TO CHRIST**.*

2 Corinthians 11:3

who stole
your identity?

Have you been hacked?
There is something worse than
having your credit card number stolen.
Or your SS number ripped off.
Or your Facebook account hijacked.

Even worse is when Satan hacks your emotions.
That's when he steals your understanding
of who you are.

Question.
What's the first thing you think about when someone
asks you the question: "who are you?"

Do you think of your job title?
Do you think of your athletic accomplishments.
Do you think of your skills or appearance?
Or maybe you think of your failures.
Maybe you think about what your dad said about you
when you were growing up.

What you think about yourself will impact your life.

When you received Jesus you got a new identity and Satan has been trying to steal it from you ever since.

The Bible says that in Jesus you have been recreated into someone new. You are chosen by God and His child forever.

Satan is first and foremost a liar and a thief.

He wants nothing more than to steal your true identity in Christ by lying to you.

He knows he can discourage you by getting you to doubt who God made you.

So I ask you...

Who.
Are.
You?

God says you are...

A new creation
His kid
Forgiven
Free
Heir of God
Royal priest
Chosen
In Christ
Alive

So what do YOU say?
(HINT: Just agree with Him.)

*You (pharisees) are of your father the **DEVIL,** and your will is to do your father's desires. He was a murderer from the beginning, and does **NOT STAND IN THE TRUTH**, because there is **NO TRUTH** in him. When he **LIES**, he speaks out of his own character, for he is a **LIAR** and the **FATHER OF LIES**.*

John 8:44

fish 'n chips

Sometimes a building is in such bad shape that it cannot be remodeled. It has to be torn down so that a brand new one can be built.

There is a Long John Silvers fast food restaurant near where we grew up. It has been there since the 70's. Many years ago, though, I was driving down the road and noticed the building had been torn down – completely down to the ground.

It was gone!

A few weeks later, I drove down the same road and noticed a new building was going up. To my surprise, I discovered that they were building a new Long John Silvers restaurant that looked just like the first one.

It did not seem to make much sense. Why would you go to the cost of destroying a restaurant in order to turn right around and build another just like it?

What I eventually learned was that the original building had become infested with some type of insects. It was so bad, that the building could not be repaired.

It had to be completely destroyed.

Some things cannot be fixed. They have to be replaced.

That is what the death and resurrection of Jesus Christ was all about.

We inherited a sinful nature from
our great, great….great grandpa Adam.

It was in our genes.
The sin problem was not just a surface problem.
It went all the way down to our spiritual roots.
That sinful nature affected everything we tried to do.

We could not be fixed.
We had to be replaced.

When Jesus died on the cross, He not only died for our sins (plural), He also took our old sinful nature to the cross. The old self-centered race of Adam was nailed to the tree and put to death. When He arose, He started a brand new race of people who would have a new nature on the inside. His Spirit would live inside our heart.

The work of Jesus is both one, big demolition project
and one, big construction project.

On the cross, He demolished our old nature.
The empty tomb is the birth of our new nature.

ON THIS SIDE OF THE CROSS,
Christ is not trying to fix the old you.
He has made you new.

Therefore, if ANYONE

is in Christ,

he is a

~~better person~~

~~religious person~~

~~much improved person~~

NEW CREATION.

The old has passed away;

behold, the new has come.

2 Corinthians 5:17

42

good news: you died!

One of my responsibilities as a basketball dad for my youngest son's team was to keep stats during the games on an iPad. There is a cool app that makes it easy. We keep record of pretty much everything every player does, good or bad. Missed shots, made shots, rebounds, fouls, steals, turnovers, blocks, etc. all get recorded on the iPad for future generations to see. When a player comes out of the game, however, we no longer keep record of anything they do.

They are, in effect, dead to the game.

God is not keeping stats on us on a cosmic iPad.
We are out of the game entirely.
We got taken out of the game
when Christ took our death for us.
He did not just take my sins to the cross.
He took me, the sinner, to the cross as well.

Many times, when we think about God's grace being free and undeserved, we usually think about it in terms of God not keeping record of the bad things we do.

He does not hold our sins against us.
That is true.

We know that our old self was **CRUCIFIED** with him

Romans 6:6

So you also must consider yourselves **DEAD** to sin and alive to God in Christ Jesus

Romans 6:11

Likewise, my brothers, you also have **DIED** to the law through the body of Christ

Romans 7:4

I have been **CRUCIFIED** with Christ. It is no longer I who live

Galatians 2:20

For you have **DIED**, and your life is hidden with Christ in God

Colossians 3:3

We all know that Jesus died for us on the cross. That's only part of the good news, though. What is not so well known is that **WE DIED WITH HIM!**

When He died, we died!

Once you are dead, you no longer do good or bad.
A dead person does not do anything – good or bad.

In the days of slavery in the U.S., many of the songs that came out of that tragic condition spoke of heaven and life after this world. Sadly, for many, the only way out of slavery was to die. The same is true spiritually. The only way to be free from slavery to sin is to die.

The good news is that spiritually we already died with Christ on the cross. Through our death with Christ, we have been set free.

Freedom from the destruction of sin does not come by trying harder to be more committed.

Freedom comes through our death with Christ.

Dying with Jesus is NOT something we need to make happen.
It has already been done!
It is a present reality for us to believe.

The good news is:
YOU DIED!

[random]
"I'm not all that spiritual, but I have a Savior who is. And that's enough."

why I'm not a follower of Jesus

I do not describe myself as a "follower" of Jesus.

Before you brand me a heretic and burn me at the stake, let me explain.

When Jesus of Nazareth walked physically on the Earth, the disciples and others followed Him. They literally followed Him around as He strolled through Galilee and other places. Jesus had not yet died and risen from the dead.

He had not yet sent His Holy Spirit to live in them. Without His Spirit, the best option was to literally follow Him around.

AFTER the cross and resurrection, Jesus floated up in the air and disappeared into the sky. Then, He sent His Holy Spirit to live inside of us. Believers became one with Him.

*From now on, therefore, we regard no one according to the flesh. Even though we once regarded Christ according to the flesh, **WE REGARD HIM THUS NO LONGER**.*

2 Corinthians 5:16

They no longer followed Him like they did before the cross.

That is why the New Testament says
we are members of His body.
The phrase that is constantly used
after the death and resurrection is "in Christ."

We are in Christ and He is in us.
That is much better than just following Him.

You follow someone else when you are a separate person.
When you are one with Christ, you do not follow Him.
He lives through you.

In his second letter to the folks at Corinth,
Paul said something amazing about Jesus.

He said that he used to view Jesus according to "the flesh."
But no longer.

He was talking about the natural, physical person called Jesus of
Nazareth. (You know, the Bearded/Sandaled One.)

Paul goes on to say that he does NOT view Christ that way anymore.
In that same passage, he talks about living by faith and focusing on the
things that are spiritual and eternal.

The point is this: Even though Paul lived at the same time
as the Bearded/Sandaled One,
He considered it much more important to know the resurrected Christ.

It is good to learn about the Bearded/Sandaled One who was God in
human flesh, but there is no life in that intellectual knowledge.

Real life and freedom comes as we know the eternal Son of God who lives today in our heart.

This is NOT a matter of semantics!
It is the difference between living under the hex and living in freedom.

You are in Christ and He is in you.
That is better than just being a follower
of the Bearded/Sandaled One.

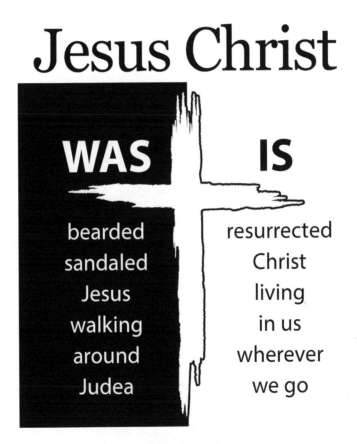

Jesus Christ

WAS   **IS**

bearded   resurrected
sandaled   Christ
Jesus   living
walking   in us
around   wherever
Judea   we go

...Even though we
ONCE REGARDED CHRIST
ACCORDING TO THE FLESH,
WE REGARD HIM THUS NO LONGER.

2 Corinthins 5:16

busted by Chloe's people!

Apparently, Chole's bunch didn't appreciate the fussing by some of the believers. They had been arguing over who FOLLOWED who. Paul called them out.

> *I appeal to you, brothers, by the name of our Lord Jesus Christ, that all of you agree, and that there be no divisions among you, but that you be united in the same mind and the same judgment. For it has been reported to me by CHLOE'S PEOPLE that there is quarreling among you, my brothers. What I mean is that each one of you says, "I follow Paul," or "I follow Apollos," or "I follow Cephas," or **"I FOLLOW CHRIST."** Is Christ divided? Was Paul crucified for you? Or were you baptized in the name of Paul?*

1 Corinthians 1:10-13

Paul did NOT endorse the group claiming to "follow Christ." He didn't say, "Yeah, you're the group who gets it right."

It seemed Paul was not wild about that phrase. It was not one he ever promoted.

Well, that's interesting.

Way to go, Team Chloe!

swingin'
emotions

Emotions are part of being human.
Some days you are up.
Some days are down.
Faith in Jesus stabilizes your emotions somewhat,
but you can/will have mood swings.

Feelings are real.
While we need to accept them,
we shouldn't let them run our lives.

It's like being on a swing set.
Feelings will sway back and forth.
But in Jesus we are still secure and connected at the top,
where the connection stays put.
The top connection of the swing never moves.
It stays attached.

There are days when you FEEL apart from God.
But the connection with Jesus is still attached.

[
There are bad days when everything goes wrong.
You FEEL as though God isn't even aware of you.
But the connection with Jesus is still attached.
]

Don't let your emotions freak you out.
You will swing back and forth at times.

Any number of things can effect you emotionally...

lack of sleep
sickness
exhaustion

Heck, if your dog runs away from home you're going to feel a bit down about that.

Feelings go UP.
Feelings go DOWN.

But none of this changes your connection to God through Jesus.

It's just life on this planet.

Remember your connection with God is always intact.
The swing is NOT coming down.
You are still attached through Jesus.

IV.

How Grace
Sets You Free

*To him who **LOVES** us and has*
FREED** us from our sins by his **BLOOD

Revelation 1:5

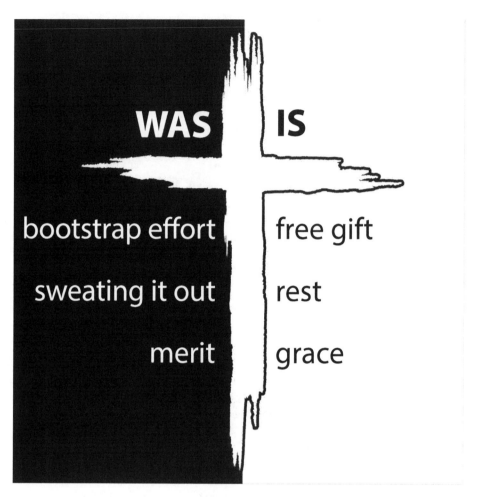

The cross released God's grace in a new way.

Jesus plays the game through us

Christianity is unique. It is the only way of living where the One who instructs us is also the power inside of us who carries out the instruction.

Michael Jordan was the greatest basketball player of all time. He later became a coach. He taught. He inspired. He ran the practices. He did everything he could to make his players the best possible.

There was one thing he could NOT do:
he could not play the game through them.

But that is EXACTLY what Jesus does.

He plays the game through us.

If we read the teachings of Jesus
without keeping the cross in clear focus,
we will misunderstand what Jesus meant.

(It happens ALL the time.)

Without the cross in view, the teachings of Jesus are just moral ethics with **NO POWER**.

The ministry of Jesus took place between the old way of keeping laws and the new way of life through Him. His teachings were during a time of transition.

You therefore must be **PERFECT**, *as your heavenly Father is* **PERFECT**.

Matthew 5:48

For by a single offering he has **PERFECTED** *for all time those who are being sanctified.*

Hebrews 10:14

People who depend on their own goodness pretend
to be holy
to be moral
to be something they are not to impress others.

[
**Self-effort produces temporary results on the outside;
grace produces lasting results on the inside.**
]

Grace teaches us to say, "NO" to sin, not "YES."

People who understand grace may sin,
but grace eventually lets the air out of sin.

In the long run they discover that faith in the finished work of Jesus and relationship with God the Father is far better than sin. You don't need to use rules to hammer away at sin to loosen its grip on your life. Grace will do that. Grace TRAINS us away from sin.

Grace weakens sin's grip and strengthens God's grip.

The more you become absorbed in God's grace toward you, the more your affections move toward Him and away from destructive actions and attitudes. Sin becomes less enticing.

Thank your Father in heaven each day for His grace. He is an infinitely gracious Father who is committed to you.
He loves you.

Experiencing His grace weakens the grip of sin.

It's easier to sin against rules
than to sin against God's love.

that is sooooo 1st century b.c.

There's an old way to serve
and a new way to serve.

The OLD WAY obligated you to serve because it said so in the scripture.

That's the way we tended to operate.

We told people to evangelize because the Bible says
"go into all the world and preach the Gospel."
Case closed.

The Bible said you should do it,
so you should do it.
Period.

You should tithe because the Bible says
"bring all the tithes into the storehouse."
Case closed.
The Bible commands us to tithe.
Just do it.

That's the way it worked:
it's written down so do it.
[NOT so fast.]

On this side of the cross
we have the Holy Spirit living in us.

He leads.
He guides.

Now we serve,
not under obligation,
because someone can find a verse,
but because the Holy Spirit guides us.

Big difference.

(and it's been this way since the first century A.D.)

OLD

because
it says
so right here,
buddy

NEW

because
the
Spirit of God
leads

*...written
not with ink
but with the
SPIRIT of the
living God,
**NOT ON
TABLETS OF
STONE** but
**ON TABLETS
OF HUMAN
HEARTS**....*

*...who has
made us
sufficient to
be ministers
of a new
covenant, not
of the **LETTER**
but of the
SPIRIT. For
the **LETTER**
KILLS, but the
SPIRIT GIVES
LIFE.*

2 Corinthians 3:3,6

dripping faucet

Do you ever feel that if you were a "better Christian,"
then God would be more ready and willing
to bless you and work on your behalf?
Sometimes we have a wrong view of God.
Actually, much of the time.
For some of us, pretty much all of the time.

We think He is waiting to see how committed we are before He really starts to move in our favor.

Many years ago when I was a newlywed, I encountered my very first plumbing problem. The kitchen faucet was dripping. It seemed to be in my job description to fix it. It was frustrating. No matter how I positioned the handle or how hard I pushed it down, the drips of water insisted on coming out. I had never dealt with this before. In that pre-Google era, I honestly did not understand why the water would not stop dripping.

It was a revelation to me that evening when I realized that there was pressure behind the water forcing it out. I had never understood that turning on the faucet did not MAKE the water come out. Turning on the faucet simply opened the path to let it come out.

I also remember thinking, "So, that's why
they put water towers way up in the air!"

The point is this: Many of us tend to view God's work in our lives the way
I used to view the water in the pipe. We mistakenly think that God is
neutral at best and it is up to us to pull out His grace.

**We think God's work
in our lives depends on:**

**OUR commitment
OUR devotion
OUR effort
OUR knowledge
OUR whatever...**

(BIG YIKES!!!)

THAT is the hex!

We don't realize that He has already worked, and is working, in our lives.

We do NOT have to do ANYTHING to get Him on our side and to
experience His love. The pressure is already there from His side.

It is our self-effort that stops the flow.

On this side of the cross,
all we do is receive
His love.

The pressure is already there from His side.
It is our self-effort that stops the flow.

zombie zone

Jesus didn't come to make bad people good, but to make dead people alive.

(Not sure who originally said this but I wish it had been me.)

Jesus did not come to merely modify our behavior. He did NOT come to bring better principles for living, or religious rules.

He came to give us life, His life. He came to make us truly alive in Him.

Think of it like this: before receiving Jesus we were like zombies. We were the walking dead. We went through the motions of living, but we did not live deeply.

Jesus is our life.
He is our full and satisfying life.

He has no intention of robbing you of truly living. He did not die so you could live out a miserable existence. He did not give His life to you so you could merely make it to the 10:30 service.

And with His life in you, one thing changes immediately: your ability to hear/respond to your Father in heaven.

Your relationship with Him comes alive.
YOU come alive.

WAS

IS

dead
in
sins

alive
in
Christ

V.

How Our Father Adores You

*Consider the kind of **EXTRAVAGANT LOVE**
the **FATHER** has lavished on us—
He calls us **CHILDREN OF GOD!**
It's true; we are His **BELOVED CHILDREN**.*

1 John 3:1 (The Voice)

WAS | IS

God | God
Abba
Father

The crucifixion of Jesus opened the way
for God to become our personal Father.

a world
of orphans

Every one of us desperately longs
to be loved by a father.

None of us, including my children,
have a perfect earthly father.

Apart from Christ, we miss out on the love of our
perfect Heavenly Father. Most Christians do not
experience the reality of God's affection day to day.

We live in a world of orphans.

To one degree or another, we were all orphans.
Just about every problem in the world today can be
traced back to the fact that people are missing the
love of God the Father.

Without the love of Abba Father, we act like orphans.

An orphan can easily feel insecure.

Orphans may feel like no one really cares about them
so they have to watch out for themselves. Often,
an orphan is used to being let down and rejected.
Many orphans do not know where tomorrow's food

is coming from so they live in fear. They may hoard extra food or clothes or money because they have no father to provide for them. They learn to trust no one. They live with the idea that they have to make their own way in life.

Many believers go through life as if they are spiritual orphans.

They live out of fear of not doing enough to get God's blessings. They strive to do better as if it all depends on their own performance. They know little of the generosity of their Heavenly Father.

The night before Jesus was crucified He told His disciples (grown men) that He would not leave them as orphans. Striking!

He went on to say that He would send His Spirit to live in us.
Jesus came to show us the Father.
He came to bring us into a relationship with our Heavenly Father.

His Spirit lives within us and cries out, "Abba, Father!"

You are no longer an orphan.

In Christ, you have a Father in Heaven who is absolutely crazy about you. Come to Him each day as your Father. You have a heavenly Father who cares for you and provides for you. It is one thing to know that as a fact in your head. It is something else to actually experience His love in your spirit.

Ask Father to make His love known to you.
Ask Him to release His love in you through His Spirit.

He is a perfect Father who delights in giving good gifts to His children.

Father God is more pleased with you than you are of your self.

Jeremiah Johnson
@gracepoint555

nascar christianity

I am not a NASCAR fan. I do not have anything against it. I have good friends who are really into it. I love sports, but for some reason, auto racing does not interest me.

I know enough about NASCAR, though, to kind of understand how it works. There is a big track that is shaped somewhat like an oval or some similar geometric shape. All the cars lineup, give it the gas, keep turning left and go round and round until someone finally goes around a certain number of times faster than everyone else. I do appreciate its simplicity.

It is a road, however, that leads nowhere. There is no destination. You just go round and round and end up where you started. Technically, I guess, it's not a road. It is a track. An actual road leads to someplace. A road is not an end in and of itself. It is a means to get somewhere.

For many people, their relationship with Jesus is like a NASCAR track. It does not go anywhere. They just go in circles. Many believers know Christ as their eternal Savior, but have not continued on through Christ to have a genuine, intimate relationship with God as their Father.

Jesus said that He is THE way. A way is a road. If He is the Way, where does He lead?

He said that He is the Way to the Father and that no one comes to the Father any other way other than through Him. Knowing Jesus Christ is not an end in and of itself. He did not come and die for us and rise again just so we would know Him.

Jesus came to bring us to the Father.

He wants you to know the love of the Father just as He knows the love of the Father. He did not just come to deliver you from Hell. I often just saw that verse about Him being "the way" as having to do with how to get to Heaven. That is not primarily what Jesus is talking about. He is the means to come to God, not just as God, but specifically as YOUR FATHER.

Jesus Christ is not a NASCAR track that leads nowhere. He is the road to a destination. That destination is the love of Abba Father.

Our Heavenly Father longs for you to walk with Him as His child. We come to Father through the Son, Jesus Christ.

Imagine that I load up my car to go on a trip and someone sees me and asks, "Where are you going?" Then, I say "Interstate 75, then Interstate 40." That would not make sense. We do not go on a road as a destination. We go on a road to get someplace else. Jesus also described Himself as a door. The purpose of a door is to enter into a different place. Jesus is the door to the Father.

The goal of the Christian life is not just to know Jesus more and more. Don't misunderstand me. It is good to know Christ more and more, but that is not the final destination. The heart of the good news of Jesus Christ is that THROUGH HIM, we can know THE FATHER! You were created to experience the affection of your Father in Heaven here and now. Jesus is the only way there.

you do <u>not</u>
_{merely}matter to God

Imagine on Valentine's Day the love of your life, your sweetheart, gives you a card. You open it up and read, "you matter to me." Would that thrill you? Would that warm your heart? Probably not.

Why do we say things like that and dilute God's love for us? God LOVES you! That goes way beyond our flimsy thoughts about how we think of God's feelings for us.

God is not merely CONCERNED for you.
God is not merely THINKING about you.
You do not merely MATTER to God.
God does not merely CARE about you.
GOD IS CRAZY IN LOVE WITH YOU.

He is obsessed with you!

If the prodigal son "mattered" to his father then his dad would have waited until his son reached the house, opened the door, listened to his son's offer to become a servant and then offered him a job at $15.00 an hour. He would have said, "OK, then, fix the fence on the back forty and here's the key to the bunk house." Instead, he tackled him with hugs and kisses, then threw a party to celebrate his return.

That is how God feels about YOU.
You more than matter to Him.

The shorter the prayer, the greater the faith. *"Help!"* is a great prayer.

Andrew Wommack
@andrewwommack

this time...
it's personal

My life (Jeff) forever changed on January 21, 2014 in a very good way.

It was on that day that our daughter gave birth to our first grandchild, Elizabeth. We, of course, had been expecting the happy event for several months, but I had not really expected what it would feel like the first time I saw this precious little person.

When I saw Elizabeth for the first time, there was an immediate feeling of attachment that was absolutely amazing. I felt affection for her that I did not know I could feel. I do not know how many thousands of babies were born into the world that day, but for me, there was only one.

The moment I first laid eyes on this little girl, I knew that I would be more than willing to lay down my life for her if needed.

THAT is how your heavenly Father feels about you RIGHT NOW.

Actually, His feelings for you are even stronger than that.

For as long as I can remember, I have been told God loves me. If asked, I would have said I believed

notes

Chapter 2
1. P.T. Forsythe, *The Cruciality of the Cross*,
(Hodder and Stoughton, 1908)

Chapter 38
1. Wayne Jacobsen, *He Loves Me!*,
(Windblown Media, 2007), 43

Chapter 46
1. Watchman Nee, *The Normal Christian Life*,
(Tyndale House Publishing, Inc., 1977), 156

Chapter 48
1. Brennan Manning, *The Ragamuffin Gospel*,
(Multnomah Books, 2005)

Chapter 55
1. Watchman Nee, *The Normal Christian Life*,
(Tyndale House Publishing, Inc., 1977), 168-169

Chapter 70
1. Brennan Manning, *The Ragamuffin Gospel*,
(Multnomah Books, 2005)

Roger Fields
by Jeff Fields

Roger is the older and less athletic of the Fields brothers. After several years in vocational ministry with congregations in Kentucky and Florida, he founded Kidz Blitz Ministries. With Kidz Blitz, he has led high-energy events in children's, youth and family Ministries for congregations in over 50 denominations across America.

Roger is the husband of his wonderful wife, Lori, and the dad of four beautiful daughters. Roger and Lori live on and manage a wedding farm in Nicholasville, KY. He drives a pick-up truck and likes to pretend he is a real farmer. He does not play golf and has an unhealthy, condescending attitude toward those who do.

Jeff Fields
by Roger Fields

Jeff is the younger and less creative of the Fields brothers. Jeff is a wonderful husband and fantastic father of six amazing kids. He works in the financial services industry out of his fancy-schmancy office in downtown Lexington, Kentucky. He wears a coat and tie most every day.

He has an amazing sense of humor and a keen intellect. His ministry background as a former pastor combined with his business experience provides refreshing perspective in real life issues. Jeff is well-balanced, more so than me, except that he golfs way too much with his rich friends.

Roger and Jeff are both recovering pastors with no history of scandal.

once upon a time

Roger's wife, Lori, had been asking him for some time to write a book about Jesus' love for us. She wanted something simple that even non-readers would pick up and enjoy. "I want something edgy," she would say. "It has to catch your eye, draw you in and keep your interest." Roger resisted. "Writing is hard work," he complained. She continued saying, "I know God wants this for His children to help them know that He Loves them. They don't have to work for it or earn it." She wanted this as a written legacy for her children, something they could hold in their hand to remind them of Gods love when things get tough. Finally, God put it on Roger's heart to pursue it on one condition: that his brother, Jeff, would write it with him.

Roger and Jeff had been talking for months about their new understanding of God's love and grace. Coming from different spiritual vantage points and with different life experiences, they had arrived at many of the same conclusions.

So one day Roger called Jeff and said, "I have a project for you. Let's write a book together." Jeff immediately agreed. They began to work. Their big challenge was to keep the book from becoming too theological. "We don't want to write it for people like us," Jeff would say.

Hundreds of hours and conversations later, this book emerged.

Listen to **The Fields Brothers Show** podcast for a light-hearted take on life in Kentucky and their thoughts about enjoying life on this side of the cross.

(Available on iTunes.)

contact info

Visit us on the web
breakingthehex.com

Like us on Facebook
facebook.com/breakingthehex

Email Roger and Jeff at
fieldsbrothers@breakingthehex.com

Broken Egg Press
2308 Lakeside Dr.
Lexington, KY 40502

ask us about discount pricing
for bulk orders of 10 or more